Pirate Gold

Elisabeth Beresford

Illustrated by Rhiannon Powell

OXFORD

UNIVERSITY PRESS

A long time ago Rob and his sister, May, lived with their family on the small island of Riduna. One day they were looking after their goats down by the bay when a sea mist drifted in.

Soon they could hardly see anything. Suddenly,
Rob, who had very sharp ears, said, "Listen!"

They could hear voices floating across the water.
They peered through the mist and could just see a
ship with a black flag.

"It's a pirate ship!" whispered May.

As the ship moved closer, the mist curled away. Rob and May could see pirates running backwards and forwards along the deck. The ship seemed to be in trouble.

There was a lot of shouting, then another noise.
SPLASH, SPLASH, SPLASH!
The pirates were throwing things into the sea.

"Quick! Run and get help," whispered Rob. "I'll stay here."

May ran back to the village as fast as she could. The goats trotted behind her.

"Shush!" she whispered. "Pirates can be VERY dangerous!"

Rob crouched behind a tall rock. He could just see a small rowing boat being lowered into the water. Four pirates climbed down into it and began to row towards the shore. They were arguing over a large map which they kept turning round and round.

The boat landed close to Rob's rock. He was so
scared that he could hardly breathe. The pirates
began to walk across the sand, but suddenly they
stopped. A bleating sound was coming from behind
a rock.

One of the goats had stayed behind, and was nibbling at Rob's jacket.

"Oh no!" thought Rob, holding his breath.

One of the pirates came striding up to him.

"Hi there, lad," said the pirate. "Can you help us? We don't know where we are."

Rob breathed again.

"We got lost in the mist," said the pirate, "and drifted towards the island by mistake. We thought we were going to hit the rocks because we were so low in the water. We had to throw some of our cargo overboard."

So the pirates had come to Riduna by mistake. Rob was relieved. The islanders were very poor, so if the pirates had come for money, they had none to give them.

When May reached the village, her father was surprised to see her.

"Why have you come home early? Where's Rob?" he asked. May was out of breath.

"P-p-pirates!" she panted.

Her father stared at her, then ran to the big bell in the church tower.

CLANG, CLANG, CLANG!

The clanging bell meant trouble and people came rushing out of their houses and barns. Out in the fields they stopped work and ran back to the village.

They all crowded round May while she told them
about the pirate ship down at the bay.

"Quick, we must go and rescue Rob," said
her father.

The islanders grabbed poles, sticks and spades and ran down to the bay. When they got there, there was no sign of Rob and the pirate ship had vanished.

"The pirates must have kidnapped Rob!" said May, starting to cry. Her father put his arm round her and everyone looked very worried.

But Rob was perfectly safe. In fact, he was enjoying himself because he was guiding the pirate ship safely out of the bay. The pirates had thrown so many heavy things overboard that the ship was now light enough to sail over the rocks beneath the sea.

As they left the rocky shore behind them, the mist cleared and the sun came out.

"Thank you, lad," said the Pirate Captain. "You've saved us and our ship. Why don't you stay with us? You could become a pirate and make your fortune!"

For a moment Rob felt excited by the idea, but then he thought of his family and friends.

"Thank you very much," said Rob, "but I belong on the island."

"Well, take this for all your trouble then," said the Captain, and he dropped something round and heavy into Rob's hand. Rob's eyes grew round too. Clutched in his hand was a shining gold coin.

Rob put the coin inside his belt and did it up tightly to keep it safe. Then he looked back at the shore. It was getting further and further away.

He must go before it vanished for ever. He climbed
onto the ship's rail, then dived overboard.

"Here he comes, here he comes!" shouted May, jumping up and down on the shore. As Rob stumbled out of the sea, the islanders crowded round him.

They were glad to have him back safe and sound.
Rob's father put a cloak round his shoulders, then
everyone sat down to hear what had happened.

At the end of Rob's story the islanders were silent. They could hardly believe what they had heard. Then Rob's father said, "Perhaps the pirates threw some of their treasure overboard. Now that the tide is out we could go and have a look!"

But it wasn't treasure that they found. It was pots
and pans, benches and chairs, great big heavy plates
and mugs, bits of wood, old guns and cannons.

The islanders were delighted. This was even better than treasure because they could use every single thing. One man wanted a bench for his workshop and here it was! Somebody else had only one plate left in their house, so the family had been taking turns to use it.

A third islander, who was very clever at making things, said that he could turn the wood and cannons into pipes and a barrel so that the next time it rained they could all have fresh water.

Everyone was so pleased with their treasure that they decided to have a party on the beach. Everyone, that is, except for Rob and May.

They were so tired after all the excitement that
they had curled up in a warm sand dune and gone to
sleep. Safely in Rob's hand lay the gold coin.

For Rob, that was the best bit of all the pirate treasure – pirate gold!